Body Talk

Other great books to get your hands on

Anita Naik

Am I Normal?
Families: can't live with them, can't live without them!
Is this Love?
The 'Just Seventeen' Quiz Book

Adele Lovell

The 'Just Seventeen' Guide to being Gorgeous

Helen Benedict

Stand up for Yourself!

Victoria McCarthy

Don't just sit there – Get a Life!

Charlotte Owen

Everything you ever wanted to know about periods...
but didn't like to ask!

(To find out more about these books, turn to page 128.)

Body Talk

by

Victoria McCarthy

Illustrations by
Alison Fleming

h
Hodder
Children's
Books

a division of Hodder Headline plc

With love to The Muswell Hill Billies (Karon, Graeme, Alex, Laura, Mike,
Kyle, Steve, Rob, Jiouxleigh, Marc, Marco and Giuseppe).
"Stick the kettle on. I'll be there in fourteen hours!"

Immeasurable thanks to: Anne Clark, Lyn Coutts, Anita Naik
(as always) and Anna and Cal McCarthy.

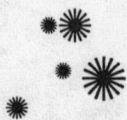

Text copyright © 1997 Victoria McCarthy

The right of Victoria McCarthy to be identified as the author of the work has been asserted by her
in accordance with the Copyright, Designs and Patents Act 1988.

Illustrations copyright © 1997 Alison Fleming
Design by Maria D'Orsi at Wilson Design Associates
Published by Hodder Children's Books 1997

10 9 8 7 6 5 4 3 2 1

ISBN 0 340 67086 X
Printed by Cox and Wyman

Hodder Children's Books
A division of Hodder Headline plc
338 Euston Road
London NW1 3BH

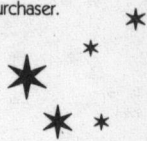

More about Victoria

We last left Victoria sitting under a shady umbrella on the west coast of Mexico. (If you didn't know that, you obviously didn't read her last book 'Get A Life', so get to it!) Victoria has travelled a long way since she gave up her job as a reporter on the 'Hartlepool Evening Mail' and moved to digs in London to work on 'Just Seventeen' magazine. Anyway, Vic-babe is on the move again. She's put a 'To Rent' sign on her umbrella, packed her sombrero and is heading for the Outer Hebrides (Look it up!).

Knowing how much she loved Mexico, nothing but a shortage of concealer stick, liquorice allsorts or her mother would have made her leave, unless it had something to do with love. Whether it was an abundance of unwanted attention, or no attention at all that has driven her ever northward, she's not telling. But if you read between the lines of Victoria's latest book (the one in your hands) you may just find out.

Contents

Introduction

Body Language
The power to move

Imagine you're in a dream world where pop stars write YOU love letters, Ben and Jerry's ice-cream is calorie-free, and Arsenal isn't a boring football team. Into this Utopia walks the Good Fairy of World Peace to grant you a wish.

The Good Fairy's job is to help the people of the world communicate, and to encourage nation to speaketh unto nation. So the wish she can grant is limited by her job description; the gift of the gab is a cert, but fast cars and hot dates are a no-no.

In a gentle yet firm manner the Good Fairy leads you into your school language laboratory and pushes you into a wobbly orange plastic chair. (Whoa! What happened to dream land?)

"*Right*, buddy," says the fairy, "today I'm going to do you one huge-type favour and give you the gift of total fluency in any language you choose.

If you want to speak Swahili I'll just wave my wand and it shall be done. You want to parler français? Then in a blinding flash of Jean-Michel Jarre laser light, fluent French will all be yours. So, go ahead — pick a language."

Now which language would you choose? Would you go for a bit of Swedish so that you can Internet with Abba? Would you opt for Russian because the B.B.C.

8

always needs Russian-speaking journos for Moscow? Nah.
I'll tell you what you'd do (if you had any sense, that is),
you'd say adiós to Español, bid arrivederci to Italiano, and
forget all about français. You'd look the Good Fairy straight
in the eye (she only has one) and lay it on the line.

"Okay, fairy babe, here's my wish. I want to learn body
language, so that I can understand people beyond what
they actually say."

On hearing your choice the fairy has a coughing fit, turns
red in the face and disappears in a puff of smoke.
Fairies are like that, but don't despair. You've not blown
your wish because I will teach you body language. In the
interests of speed and efficiency let's replace the words 'body
language' with the initials 'B.L.' That okay with you?

The reason you have so wisely chosen B.L. is because
B.L. is used by people all over the world, in every
town, in every country, on every continent and, probably, in
most of the major solar systems. It's a language without
tedious vocabulary lists, complicated verb tables, and there's
definitely no block tests.

When you're totally clued-up on the language of bod,
you will understand what people are really all about.

The only thing you learn via the chin-wagging languages is what people want you to know. If someone tells you they love you, you have no choice but to believe them. But with B.L. you can find out the deep-down truth. In an instant you'll know if someone really truly lurves you or not. Your mum won't be able to hide her feelings any more, and if someone has it in for you, you'll be onto their game pronto.

The best bit of all is that no one will know that you're wise to them. Fluency in B.L. is like being psychic. You can see things that others can't. It's just about the best magic trick in the world!

10

By now you're consumed with uncontrollable excitement. A smile as wide as the English Channel has spread across your face and your eyes are sparkling. You sink to your knees, your arms stretched out in front. You're begging to know more about body language. Well, get a grip girlie, because I've got good news for you — you're using body language already!

Are you ready to rumble and to bodily go where few have gone before? Then simply take this page between the thumb and index finger, lift and turn. A world stranger than 'Northern Exposure' awaits you.

Chapter One

The Silence of the Limbs

It's Saturday afternoon (okay, so it's not *really* Saturday arvo but could you just use your imagination for a moment?) and you're sitting on the terraces of St James Park, Tyneside watching the world's greatest footy team, Newcastle United, strut their stuff. Your ears are covered by a pair of fluffy pink ear-muffs and you can't hear a thing. The only way you can tell how your fellow supporters feel is by looking at them.

Ten minutes into the game and the bloke next to you screws his face in a pained expression, hits his forehead repeatedly with one hand, and with the other points to the Newcastle striker. Is there a wasp on the man's forehead? Is he trying to tell the striker that there's a wasp on his forehead? Of course not.

You know instantly that your fellow supporter is peeved with the Geordie player. He is slapping his forehead:

☞ to make sure he's awake. Surely such a stupid play is the stuff of nightmares?

☞ because he can't reach out and knock some sense into the striker; and

☞ because his mental and emotional stability has been severely tested.

When he points to the striker he is making certain that everyone knows exactly which player is causing him such distress. Without saying a word, this man has clearly expressed his opinion and with it a whole flurry of emotions. See? No words. Heaps of body language. Much understanding.

At the same game you see lots of other B.L. signals: fists punched into the air to express extreme pleasure at one being put into the net; eyebrows

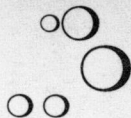

raised in horror at foul play; and everywhere shoulders shrugged above outstretched arms in disbelief at the ref's decision. If you see two fingers raised, the meaning is blatant. This example of B.L. is not clever and not to be imitated. It's just too tacky for words.

After a piece of inspired playing by the Newcastle centre forward, the golden boy manager raises his right thumb aloft. What's he doing?

(A) Showing off his Pocahontas sticking plaster.

(B) Letting the centre forward know he is extremely pleased.

(C) Placing an order for one hot-dog and a large Coke.

If you chose **(B)**, go to the top of the league. Although the golden boy is unaware of it at the time, he is using a bit of B.L. which was first employed by the ancient Romans. Like it's thousands of years old.

13

Body language gets the thumbs up

In those heady days when Nero fiddled, Rome burned, and real men wore little white wrap-around togas, the Roman equivalent of four-four-two was a quick one-to-one fight-to-the-death in the Forum.

At the southern end would be the vicious rabid lion, and at the other, one under-fed, under-paid slave. If the slave had a lucky break in the draw, then the lion would be replaced by a muscular, well-trained gladiator with hands as large as telephone books.

The only constant in the game was the under-fed, under-paid slave who did his utmost to avoid the biggest relegation of them all – death. If the slave lived to hear the full-time hooter, the emperor could decide to spare his life by giving him the thumbs-up. But if the emperor had had a lousy/nothing-on-the-telly/wife-overspent-on-the-Barclaycard sort of day, he would give the thumbs-down sign and it would be pop-your-sandals time for the slave.

So the next time you see a golden boy manager give the thumbs-up, breathe a sigh of relief for the player on the field.

In case I haven't convinced you that B.L. is the best thing since the invention of concealer sticks, here are ten reasons to get with the lingo of the limbs.

14

1 It will make you instantly more popular with friends, rock stars and international football players.

By applying specific body language rules to your life you will be amazed, nay, stunned at the hoards of celebs who will be vying for your attention. But if the thought of Johnny Depp dropping round for tea doesn't send ripples of excitement up and down your spine, take comfort in the fact that your old pals will be queuing up to share their deepest secrets. (They'll also be lining up to find out everything you know about B.L., but you're not going to tell them, are you?) For all the info on making friends with B.L. and stickyback plastic, see chapter two.

2 You'll save time, tears and a broken heart.

And how will you do this? By instinctively knowing which boys are prepared to hang a 'Reserved for you' sign around their neck. Once you've read chapter three, Time to Boywatch, you'll be able to judge if the love god at the 7-11 is actually worth investigating.

3 Members of the opposite sex will swoon at your feet, consumed with lust and unquenchable desire – maybe.

Once you've spotted a likely love contender I'll show you how to use the sorcery of body language to force the poor unsuspecting chap to fall in love with you. For the tricks of flirting, flick to chapter four.

4 Your self-confidence will soar to an unbelievable all-time high.

Are you always the last to be chosen for the netball team? Are you picked on by the school bullies? The silent and deadly martial art of B.L. will teach you to assert yourself with class. You'll also learn in chapter five that a few little body movements can shut the door on shyness.

5 You'll get extra time on the ice-rink.

With the right body language knowledge you'll become a prize manipulator – a power you will use for

16

good, not evil. After reading chapter six you'll instinctively know the best and worst times to ask your mum and dad for a favour. And with scientific precision you will be able to turn a bad situation into a good one. Oh yeah, and you'll be able to swing an extra session on the ice, too!

6 Be transformed into a celeb gossip queen.

No longer will you have to believe what they write in those cheap'n'nasty gossip columns. B.L. know-how (chapter seven) will let you suss the real story behind the paparazzi shots. You'll know if a relationship's on the rocks, or if a couple claiming to be 'just good friends' are actually 'just good lovers'. You'll know who's with who, and who is on the date'em and dump'em list.

17

7 Do some dudewatching.

By crikey, there's more! You know those mind-numbing moments spent waiting for a bus or standing in line at the check-out? Well, they're a thing of the past. Dudewatching in chapter seven is the way to go. Turn boredom into bliss and get practice in your favourite bodily lingo by studying the movements of those nearby. You never know what might be revealed. And for those of you who don't get out much, we'll show you how to dudewatch your cat.

8 Spot a porkie pie in the wink of an eye.

By watching a person's hand movements you'll be be able to pick the Honest Johns from the Lying Lizards. With a black-belt in B.L., there's no chance of someone pulling the wool over your eyes. Training pack for truth detectives is in chapter eight.

9 Interviews and oral exams will be a doddle.

B.L., as you will discover in chapter nine, will help you win the interview game. You'll impress V.I.Ps (very important people), wow examiners and knock the socks off potential boss-type bods. Are you in awe yet?

18

10 You'll achieve world domination within 28 days.

Yeah, right. And the tooth fairy really exists.

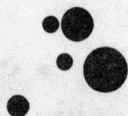

Chapter Two

How to Make Friends

A True Story — The Manhattan Reject

He was a lowly journalist sent State-side to do some interviews. She was a film star. They met at a swank restaurant in up-town Manhattan, and (sigh) love blossomed. (Well, it did for him at least.)

'He' was my mate Tony and 'she' was Meg Ryan, love goddess, movie queen and all-round clever woman, who'd met lots of starry-eyed romantic souls like Tony.

Tony flew back from New York in a daze. "Aw, maan," he said to me. "Meg was simply amazing. She was the friendliest person I've ever met! She made me feel welcome and *oooh sooo* relaxed. And you know what? She was genuinely interested in everything I said! Do you think I stand a chance?"

"Hmmm," mumbled I sceptically. "I'm very happy for you, but please realise that if you simper about this for the next twelve years I'll have to stop talking to you."

A few months later Tony, still deeply in lust, simpering and talking about it, went back to the States and – Is this boy lucky or what? – managed to score an invite to a party that Meg herself was going to attend.

This time, however, when he got off the plane back in Britain, our Tone was not a happy boy.

"She's changed," he said. "Talking to her was like talking to an entirely different person. She didn't seem interested in what I had to say, and she acted as though she didn't trust me. She even folded her arms over her chest while I was talking. She cut me out completely. What's it all mean, Vici? Has she found someone else?"

Tony was so flummoxed that we discussed this latest Meg episode and it didn't take long to work out how

and why Ms Ryan was sending out such negative messages to our Boy Blunder.

Meg, you see, was in the middle of shooting a movie in which she plays an alcoholic. And being a total professional, Meg was adopting these mannerisms in her everyday life. Yep, even when she went to a party.

When Tony thought about it, he realised that at the party Meg had walked differently and that her whole posture had changed. Now here's the crunch: Meg was using body language to help her portray a resentful alcoholic. When she folded her arms across her chest she was putting up a barrier and distancing herself. Thing is, she played her role so well that Tony was totally fooled by it. Result: Tony was a crushed and heart-broken man.

Like it or not, body language can make friendships, or break them.

A Folk Tale — The Mexican Wave

A very good example of how body language can make friendships is found thousands of miles away in Mexico. Don't know much about Mexico? Well, then let then me set you straight. It's not full of Zapata-moustached bandits, tortilla chips (from Medomsley Road, Consett) are not the only thing you'll find on a menu, and your chances of seeing a man doing siesta under, or dancing on, a sombrero are slim. Now that we've put a couple of cultural stereotypes to bed we can get on with Me-hi-co, land of *los amigos*.

Now I'm not suggesting that everyone south of the border is happy, humorous and as hospitable as a teddy on tequila (Mexico has its share of Vera Duckworth's and Cruella De Vil's), but because Mexicans use welcoming body language even the nasty bods seem friendly. Here's why:

Número uno: They smile lots.
Smiling attracts people. Smiling is friendly. Period.

Número dos: They're tactile – in all the right ways.
Even total strangers will slap you lovingly on the back and welcome you with open arms and big hugs. These gestures are automatically friend-inducing.

Número tres: They look at you.
Everybody is flattered when they meet someone who shows

real interest in what they are saying. Smiling eyeball-to-eyeball contact shows that someone has your full attention.

23

Body Alert

So, have you got the Mexican wave?

Smiling + hugging + eye contact = friendliness = many friends.

Body consciousness raising

Make a list of the people who are friendly or unfriendly toward you. Think about their B.L. and work out what it is that makes you feel comfortable or uncomfortable.

Person	Body Language
For example: Jenny	Tilts her head when I talk to her, like she's really interested.

Are you lonely tonight?

You've already discovered that some kinds of B.L. are friendlier than others, now you're going to learn the top ten body manoeuvres for making people feel instantly more relaxed in your presence.

If you learn and practise the following, I'll guarantee (well, actually I won't) that your social life will improve dramatically and existing friendships will prosper. Failing that, you'll get a few odd glances in the street. But, hey, that's life!

1 The full-frontal smile

When you were a baby you twigged very quickly that by flashing a cheesy grin at a sucker relative they were more

likely to hang around and spoil you. So, why do teen-bods (and adults, for that matter) turn their back on this attention-winning tactic? Beats me.

Smiling is so important to a very large cartoon-movie company – you know the one that has massive fantasy adventure parks all over the world and an unnatural love for a special mouse – that it actually teaches its staff to smile. Female workers are shown how to flash their top teeth, while males are tutored in the skill of revealing both sets of polished gnashers.

According to Professor S. Mirk a top teeth only smile is a caring, sharing smile that is often used between friends. The toothy male grin is a let's-have-fun one. (Haven't Disney heard that girls just wanna have fun too?)

And why does Disney go to all this trouble? Because they know it's a money-earner. If you leave Disneyland feeling that the staff liked you and that you've had a GREAT time, you're going to visit again.

Body Alert

If you're going to smile, mean it. Body language experts are quick to tell us that a wide, tight-lipped fake smile looks more like a grimace, and is off-putting. When you smile think of Keanu Reeves, a warm blue lagoon and sunshine. Then, even if your good mood is a tad faked, your smile won't be.

2 Seeing eye-to-eye

If you're going to make a new mate, you've got to see 'eye-to-eye' and show that you're really interested in everything they say. They, in turn, will be flattered.

Body Alert

Want to hide your true feelings? Then whack on a pair of shades. To impress someone with your honesty and to give real punch to what you're saying, remove the sunnies and look your friend straight in the peepers.

Body consciousness raising

Get a piece of paper about the same size as your face (a large paper bag is even better) and cut a window in it which allows you to see just your eyes and eyebrows. Put on your mask, stand in front of a mirror and let your face express the gamut of emotions from deliriously happy to depressingly sad. Notice how your eyes change with each emotion.

3 The handy-handy shake

Legend has it that hand-shaking was used in times past by gentlemen to prove that they were unarmed and came in friendship. So when you're introduced to someone for the first time let them know that you're a friendly and trustworthy

sort of person by offering your hand.

For a hand shake that says a little more – 'Not only am I honest, but I like you' – place your free hand over the person's hand-shake wrist. It's almost like shaking their one hand with both of yours. In light of its meaning don't use it on bods of the opposite sex in case they get the wrong idea.

As you get to know a person you can move your free hand further up their hand-shake arm. If you place your hand on their elbow it shows you feel more for them than if you put your hand on their wrist. If you move your hand to the upper arm or shoulder it's almost the start of a hug.

27

Body Alert

Don't use a two-handed shake in an interview situation. The interviewer may think you're being cocky!

4 Palm them off

One of the major things I look for in a new buddy is honesty. I can deal with nose-pickers, high-pitched gigglers and even people who watch 'Neighbours', but dishonesty doesn't interest me one iota. If you want to show you're honest, show off your palms. (Palms as in hands, not trees.)

Open palms are a sign of integrity. With your palms exposed anyone can see that you're not concealing a miniature love bug, stealing their ring, or hiding the last Rolo.

5 Arm-crossed lovers

When Meg Ryan crossed her arms, Tony was hurt because she was putting a barrier between herself and our Boy Blunder. But crossing your arms is not the only way to reject a suitor. You may think that crossing your legs is the ultimate lure tool, but studies have shown that it can give off negative messages like disinterest or intolerance.

28

Body Alert

The only things to cross when befriending someone are your fingers!

6 The head tilt

This trick is easy! If someone's talking to you and you are interested (or want to feign interest for decency's sake), tilt your head to one side. Don't ask me why this works, it just does.

Charles Darwin, the naturalist, noticed that animals tilted their head to one side when they were interested in something. It was then recognised that socially-successful humans did it too.

7 Talk in smiley tones

Your posture and attitude affect your voice. Slouch and you mumble; stand tall and you will speak clearly and with authority. If you smile and think happy thoughts, then you will speak in warm friendly tones. Wear a scowl and no one is going to hang around to hear what you've got to say.

8 Be a mirror image

Next time you're with someone that you want to be friendly with, 'mirror' what they do. For instance, if they lean on their left leg and push their hair behind their ears, you lean on your right leg and push your hair behind your ears. Now you might think the other person will be saying to themselves: 'Uh, oh! Freak alert. Copy cat on the loose.' But they won't be. Mirroring is a very subtle B.L. technique which subconsciously says that you are in tune with each other. If a friendship is meant to be, then it won't be long before they mirror your actions. Try it and see.

9 Sit-ups for friendship

Nought to do with flattening your tum; all to do with displaying your interest. Next time you're sitting down with

someone (especially a potential employer, examiner or boyfriend), sit up straight on the edge of your chair and face your chin-wagging partner.

Body Alert

Don't sit too far forward or you'll give the impression that you're about to get up and leave. This would send totally unfriendly messages to your would-be buddy or boss!

10 **Buy some deodorant, please!**
Well, somebody had to tell you, and your best mate wouldn't.

Body consciousness raising

You're meeting someone for the first time and you can tell that they are nervous and ill-at-ease. What can you do body-wise to make them more relaxed?

_____

_____

_____

_____

Now that you know how to make friends, it's time to learn about (cough, cough, splutter) boyfriends. Whip to chapter three for the bodily truths about the opposite sex!

Chapter Three

Time to Boywatch!

The game of love

Girl loves boy. Boy kicks football. Girl has no idea whether boy likes, loathes or loves her. Boy kicks football again. Girl vies with ball for boy's attention. Boy continues kicking football. Plan fails. Girl mopes.

The score at full-time: Football 1, Girl 0.

This, girls, is the nature of love. Every fem from Cleopatra to Hillary Clinton has been through the love dilemma: you've got a crush, you've got it *baad* and the object of your desire is oblivious to your sultry glances.

Boys are useless at reading and sending love messages. A girl could throw herself at a boy's feet (Where's your self-respect?) and put 'I love you' signs on her T-shirt and still the boy wouldn't get the drift. If the girl was extremely lucky her beloved might think she was being friendly. When it comes to the B.L. of love, boys are mortal dorks.

But let's say – and this is a far-fetched hypothesis – that the boy cottons on to

the girl's 'I really like you' message and decides he is up for a spot of l'amour; the chances are that the girl would be the last to know.

Why is that, you ask? It's because boys assume that girls are possessed of amazing psychic abilities and will automatically know when love is in the air and being propelled in their direction. Anyway, time passes and the girl continues sending smoke signals of love, but the boy does nothing (buffoon). More time passes and the boy, thinking that he was mistaken about mutual l'amour, turns his attention back to things like 'Fantasy Football'. And so ends a beautiful thang.

It seems then, that it is left to us girls to keep the merry-go-round of love turning. To find out if your Olly Oblivious fancies you, apply this test:

Question 1: Is he giving you the eye?
He's looked at you, but he's looked at Mrs White from the butchers, too. To tell the difference between '*a* look' and '*the* look' scrutinise his gaze.

The look of love lingers for a few seconds, and before looking away he will flash a smile. But before leaping to any rash conclusions, check that he is not just looking at a huge bogey hanging from your nose.

If the signs are encouraging, move a little closer and make conversation. When you're talking check out

33

his gaze. Do his eyes wander to take in other parts of your stunning anatomy? If so, you're definitely on to a good thing. This look is what anthropologists call the 'intimate' gaze, and is a totally subconscious way of checking out the rest of you while having a conversation. Tsk. Boys, eh? But come on girls, we do exactly the same thing.

Now look deeply into your boy's eyes and examine his pupils. Are they large or growing larger? Yup? Cool! This is a sign that your laddio likes what he sees.

Time for the final eye examination, and this one is so impressive you'll probably end up an optician.

Stand in front of your Hunk-from-Hades (or Halfords) and while chatting, casually notice how often he blinks. If his blink rate increases, then he's all yours, honey. Behavioural psychologists researched this one and their results were

34

conclusive: lash flutter increases when someone is looking at the one they love. Spooky!

To make absolutely certain, try this experiment. Slow down your blink rate for a while, then speed it up, and then slow it again. If the boy is tuned into you, his blink rate will be in sync with yours.

Don't despair if his blinking is hopelessly out of blinking time. He might just need practice (or glasses).

Body Alert

Do you know why love by *la luna* and candlelight is romantic? The subdued lighting makes the pupils dilate (and hides spots) and hearts go kerthump, kerthump and snog-ups ensue. Highly unhygienic, you know.

35

Question Two: Does he want to get close to you?

All humans have their own personal space – almost like a transportable aura – in which they and only they are allowed to move. If someone enters that space uninvited, the aura-owner will feel very uncomfortable.

A handful of B.L. experts have actually calculated the size of the average 'bubble' of private space people want. When you're chatting to a stranger your personal space extends just over one metre from your body. If you're talking to a friend, the bubble shrinks to

46 centimetres. The bubble almost disappears for family members and other loved ones.

So how can you use this info? Do you stand as close as you can to your crush, wait until he flinches and then whip out a ruler to measure his personal space? ('Oops. He's only let me to within 90 centimetres of him. Our relationship's got at least 50 centimetres to go.'). Perhaps not.

Try this instead: when you're next chatting to your P.B. (potential boyfriend) gradually move closer and then slowly back away. Now watch to see if your P.B. moves forward to fill the space. If he does, he wants to keep you at close quarters. The boy is hooked!

Question Three: Is he flashing at you?

There's no need to be silly. You know perfectly well that I'm not asking you if he's baring his bod in a public place. (If he is, call the police. Help is required.) The kind of flash we're concerned with here is the eyebrow flash.

Scientists have discovered that when Bod A meets a much-liked Bod B they raise their eyebrows in a gesture of recognition. Almost like drivers who flash their car's headlights when they see a friend or neat set of wheels.

Next time you're in a public place, such as a coffee bar, watch friends greeting each other. You'll be surprised at how many use the eyebrow flash. If the eyebrows don't flash they aren't good friends; won't chat for long; or the moment the other person's back is turned, will have a good bitch!

Question Four: Where are his hands?

Tsk, tsk, your naughty thoughts. Zero to do with gropes in the dark. Heaps to do with the 'he loves me, he loves me not' preening ritual.

Read the following story to see what good grooming has to do with love a'blooming.

Another True Story — Groomed for Disaster

My mate Rachel was very interested in a boy who she kept 'bumping into' all over town. Eventually the 'bumping into' happened so often that us girls in the office decided that he was in lust with Rachy-babes. But Rachel had other ideas.

37

"You're all wrong!" she sang bitterly. "You're totally, one hundred percent, completely and utterly wrong. You're all off your trolleys!"

"And pray why?" we chorused.

"Well, every time I meet him he fidgets like he's dying to get away," she said. "He's always putting his hands through his hair or straightening his jacket or something. He's really uncomfortable in my presence."

Poor Rachel couldn't see the wood for the trees. Anyone with half a brain could see that Peter (name changed to protect the innocent) was using a very common B.L. technique called 'preening'. He was tidying himself up so that he would look his best for her.

After some gentle persuasion Rachel finally got the picture and took the initiative to get the relationship going. Her advances were welcomed by Peter with open arms. We at the office breathed a communal sigh of relief.

Two weeks later Rachel stormed in saying that Peter was THE most boring individual on earth, but that she had met this other terribly nice guy!

38

Body Alert

Men who fiddle with rings or chains should be avoided. These guys are thinking about the lassie who gave them these gifts.

Question Five: Is he pointing at you?

Imagine you're sitting at a table with a group of people and your P.B. is sitting next to you. Suddenly someone grabs his attention and starts a conversation.

If your P.B. shifts his whole body toward that person then your relationship's got a way to go. By turning away he's disconnecting from you and connecting with someone else.

If, however, the P.B. only turns his head and upper body (his lower body and feet remain facing you), you can breathe a sigh of relief. Yep, he might be in deep conversation with someone else, but you're the real focus of his attention.

This is called 'body pointing' and is a sure-fire way of telling who fancies who in a group.

So, is there a snog-up in the offing or what? To find out, tally up your responses on the following check list.

39

Why not copy it and use it to keep records of every P.B. you come across? If you're anything like Rachel, you'll have gone through six lists by next Tuesday.

The 'check-him-out-checking-you-out' check list

☐ Do you catch him eyeing you off?

☐ Does he hold your gaze for a few seconds?

☐ If he makes eye contact does he smile?

☐ When he's close to you does he ever drop his gaze below your chin? (Litter lout!).

☐ Do his pupils grow large when he's with you?

☐ Does his blink rate increase when you're near?

☐ Does he blink in sync with you?

☐ When you back away does he move closer?

☐ Does he 'flash' his eyebrows when he sees you?

☐ Does he preen himself in your presence?

☐ When sitting near you does he cross his legs in your direction?

☐ When he chats is his body turned toward you?

☐ Is he free? (Just a thought.)

Score:

5 or less ~ Are you sure he's the man for you?

6 to 10 ~ Looking good.

11 to 13 ~ You've been given the look of love.

40

Chapter Four

Flirt Alert!

Signals for seduction

In the olden days before microwave chips, ink eradicators and 'Terminator I', the game of love was played with an elegant lace-edged handkerchief. Yes, you read it right – a handkerchief. To put you in the picture, let's do a bit of scene setting.

A Totally Made-up Story — S'not love, is it?

(Somewhere in Middle England in the Middle Ages)

The sound of horse hooves on the gravelled courtyard herald the arrival of the goodly knight, Sir Frederick of Thistlebottom. He's come to pay his respects, and hopefully catch a glimpse of the beautiful Princess Kylie.

Now Fred, never having heard of Michael Hutchence or witnessed the understated sensuality of Aidan Quinn, is a bit of a dodo when it comes to women, and is therefore totally unaware that the princess is quite smitten by his dashing good looks, fat bank account and pert behind.

Kylie's been waiting ages for Fred to come a'wooing, so she's going to use this opportunity to show Fred how she feels about him.

What does she do? Does she storm into the courtyard, her shapely form glued inside a shimmering pair of Azzeldine Alaia bell-bottoms, and purr "Hey Fred baby, kiss me. You know you want to!"?

Heaven forbid! This is the Middle Ages and emancipation is a long way off. Women don't even have bras to burn yet, but they do have turbo-boosted love hankies. This is what really happens.

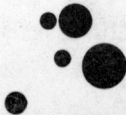

42

When Kylie saunters into the courtyard she dabs her brow with her hankie (which draws Fred's attention to her eyes which flash like deadly ray guns) and then flutters it across her face all mysterious-like. By now, Fred is drooling and breathing heavily.

Kylie then plays her trump card – she drops her hankie. Fred rushes to pick it up and hand it back, thus making her acquaintance.

What! all that hanky-waving and no hanky-panky? Sad, isn't it?

43

Fast forward to today. Kylie's castle has become a multiplex cinema, Sir Freddie's armour hangs in the Vic and Alb Museum, and hankies have been scrapped in favour of Kleenex. (Flirting with a paper towel just doesn't have the same effect.) One thing that hasn't changed: it's still not totally acceptable for women to ask men out. Why? you ask. Because females are worried about rejection, getting a bad name, and looking desperate. So instead of laying their cards on the table women flirt, or at least try to flirt.

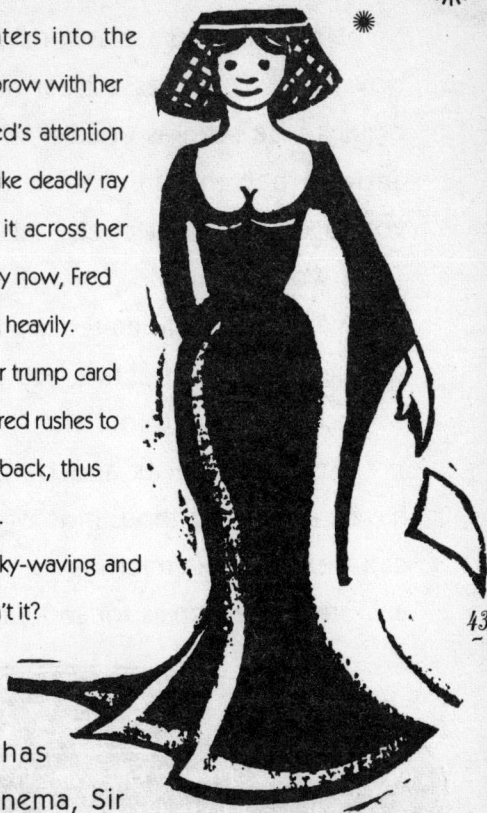

Now that lots of us girls work side-by-side with boys, we've suppressed our natural flirting abilities in order to be seen as equals. Who's got time for hankie antics when the union's on the phone asking what you're doing about cheap labour exploitation in the Third World? Hmm?

What today's liberated woman needs is a refresher course on super-effective boy-ploys. And guess what, science has come to our aid.

Anthropologists and behavioural psychologists have catalogued thousands of B.L. movements which can be used to attract mates. So take your time, vixen and study the signals for seduction.

Body Alert

Use these tips only after employing the friend-making techniques in chapter two. Best to get to know a boy before you ensnare him, huh? Obsessives can be *so* tiresome.

The language of love — signals for seduction!

Whisper sweet nothings

When you first try to woo someone it doesn't really matter what you say, it's how you say it that counts, and the trick is to say it quietly. Here's why:

If you scream at someone you really like, they'll back away – not only mentally but physically. Talk in a normal tone and your man will stand at a polite distance. But if you drop the volume way, way down he'll have no choice but to move real, real close. And before he knows it – kazam! – you've ensnared him in your personal space where he will be forced to gaze deep into your eyes and smell the sweet aroma of your skin. Cunning and clever, huh?

45

Lash appeal

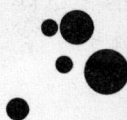

You're already clued-up on the blink rate between perfect couples, so logic will tell you that by speeding up your blink rate you will be subconsciously letting your amour know that you're interested in him.

B.L. experts also suggest that vivacious vixens and sultry seductresses should flutter their lashes in a slow two-eyed wink. Anyone who has ever seen the movie

'Roger Rabbit' will know what I'm talking about. Ultra-sexy bunny-girl, Jessica Rabbit, is expert at the slow wink. She lowers both eyelashes, and when she has the undivided attention of all and sundry she looks up and stings them with her smouldering gaze. The effect? Boys are bowled over.

In case you were wondering, winking is *not* a turn off for boys. Winking is sexy in a Drew Barrymore kind of way. It's fun and flirtatious without being heavy and serious. So if you're trying to let a boy know you're a bit of fun, wink away. (Not, however, recommended for contact lens wearers!)

46

Play hide and seek

Hide and seek – or peek-a-boo as it's sometimes called – is a teasing technique. The idea is that you look at your boy and then look away in a 'now you have me, now you don't' motion. It won't be long before your laddio-love becomes impatient and craves your full attention.

A nifty way of playing peek-a-boo is to use a magazine as a prop. Pretend to read your magazine, then gaze at your man over the top. The moment he spots you, look back at your mag (and try not to giggle). Repeat this routine three or four times. Laddio will be intrigued by your behaviour, and may even realise that he is a wanted man. Mission complete – you've got his attention.

Be a bit lippy

If you've ever wondered why we daub ourselves with lipstick and slap on rouge, wonder no more. It's a biological fact that when we fancy someone our lips and cheeks become flushed. Because of this, men find rouged lips and cheeks absolutely irresistible.

When you're playing at being Mata Hari draw your P.B.'s attention to your lips by biting your bottom lip, pouting or even chewing on a pen. However, don't go overboard or you may end up looking veritably pornographic – not a wise move. Phew.

Get necking and be 'a wristing'

Fact I: Boys are intrigued by those parts of a woman's body that they rarely get to see.

Fact II: This is why boys make such a scene when they see racy pictures of women.

Fact III: We're going to show you how to win over a boy by being revealing.

Fact IV: Don't worry, there's nothing smutty about it. All you have to lay bare are your wrists and neck.

Hard as it is to believe, lusty boys find wrists and the nape (back) of your neck incredibly sexy. Check out the adverts on T.V. and you'll see that necks and wrists are often used to make products seem sensual. Bubble bath ads feature so many necks and wrists you can't get in the tub for them.

Best thing about this bit of B.L. trickery is that you can use it anywhere, even in the classroom.

Take a seat in the row in front of your boy and gently massage the nape of your neck. Then, in the middle of a hands-on science investigation, turn your hands palm-up and gently lay one hand inside the other. Let the thumb of the bottom hand rub the exposed wrist. I can promise you the boy will be jelly for the rest of the day.

Love is in the hair

Some men like blue eyes, and others prefer brown, some men prefer long hair and others short, but all guys like to see girls playing with their hair. If you twiddle your hair around your fingers, or even suck the ends of it, your boy will be enraptured. Don't ask me why. I haven't a clue. Just take it from me that it works. Next!

Cross your legs

In the last three chapters I've been telling you not to cross anything other than your fingers for fear it's taken as a barrier when – boom! – I hit you with this: crossing your legs can make men fall head over heels in love.

Apparently there is something very alluring about the way the muscles in your calf tighten and become wonderfully shapely when you cross your legs. Your tightened muscle tone is telling the opposite sex that you're fit, healthy and confident.

The fond shoe shuffle

Some people associate shoe-fondling with fetishes, but here in body language land we know it's a method of seduction. If you cross your legs in the direction of your boy, and then let your shoe slip on and off your foot, he will take this as a sign that you are a laid-back, relaxed kind of person.

If you can shoe shuffle, expose your wrists and slow wink all at the same time, the boy will be putty in your hands before you can say 'miaow!'

49

Preen yourself

If preening worked for Peter (the most boring man on earth), just imagine what a little hair tossing can do for you. Putting on lipstick and powdering your nose is also a way of saying 'Hello boys'. Don't be afraid to glam-up in front of your boy. He'll be pleased that you want to look good for him.

50

Put the language of love into practice and your very own version of Tim Roth will be showering you with choccies and flowers. Your B.L. know-how will have him all of a quiver and it won't be long before he starts serenading you in the midnight hours.

Now that we've got the boy problem sorted out can we, perhaps, stop this boy-obsession and move onto something a *little* more substantial? Good – because the subject I want to address now is self-confidence.

Chapter Five

Confidence Tricks

How to get picked, not picked on

Me? I'm well-confident; never been nervous in my life. I can storm into a rock star's dressing room and start demanding answers without so much as blinking! I'm the type who lets people (celebs included) know when they have let me down. I once called a celluloid hero 'a pillock' when he kept me waiting four hours for an interview. I didn't even flinch when I said it. Yeah, and Madonna plays bingo in Hartlepool.

No matter what people say, no one is brimming with confidence all the time. You, the war hero, the beauty queen and Madonna have all got something in common: you're all human and have hang-ups which send your confidence running for cover.

☞ The war hero is scared of going to the dentist, despite being decorated for bravery.

52

☞ The beauty queen may seem confident (It certainly requires guts to put yourself in a beauty pageant.), but is she doing it in order to prove her own self-worth?

☞ Madonna? Well, therein lies another book. Madonna has admitted that she felt isolated and lonely as a child, and became a star in order to get some much-needed love and attention.

See? We all have our fears and foibles.

Many outward displays of bravery and bravado are really nothing more than a clever confidence trick. The next story is all about me and the getting of confidence. So, no laughing. Promise?

I remember (Danger! Warning! Anecdote ahead!) being sent as a young reporter to the studio of Tyne Tees Television to interview a couple of bands. It was the first time I'd ever met real live pop stars (as opposed to unreal dead ones) and I was shaking like a leaf. Five minutes before the first interview I was sick in the toilet. But there was worse to come. From the next cubicle came the unmistakable voice of one of the station's leading presenters.

"Crikey? Are you okay?" she asked, as I emerged from the loo, clutching my stomach.

"No," I whimpered like a jesse. "I've got to go and interview 'Bananarama' and I'm scared stiff."

"Hmmm," she smiled. "I have to interview them as well and I'm scared too."

I was gobsmacked.

"YOU? You're scared of interviewing bands?"

"Gosh, yes!" she grinned. "Last week I was interviewing Sting, and I was so nervous my voice kept breaking up. Everyone thought I had laryngitis."

"So what did you do?" I asked.

"What I always do," she said. "I stand tall and imagine that everyone in the world wants an audience with me. Then I pretend that the people I'm interviewing are my little brothers and sisters. It works a treat. You should try it."

I did, and I've never looked back (unless I'm reversing out of my drive-way).

53

Give yourself a lift — walk tall

One of the most important things the presenter shared with me was that she 'stood tall'. Feeling tall, large, high or above everyone else are key factors in the B.L. of confidence.

In the army, soldiers are drilled to walk tall with their heads held high, their chests out and shoulders back. The idea is that it gives them a sense of pride, authority and confidence.

54

And it's no small coincidence that Heads of State sit on raised thrones and are given titles like 'Your Royal *High*ness'. A similar con trick is used by court judges who sit above

the accused and other mortals, and are almost totally hidden behind the wall of panelling which surrounds their chair and desk. Not only are judges in authority, but nothing can get through their barrier of impartiality.

Get the picture? If you want to raise your self-confidence, you have to raise your body position *and* your attitude. It's not simply a matter of wearing ten inch stilettos, you also have to believe in yourself.

Body Alert
The Unbreakable Law of Confidence – If you're feeling shy, scared or nervous, breathe deeply and walk tall with your shoulders back and chin-up.

55

Master the tips on the following pages by practising them until they come naturally. If you look more confident, you'll feel more confident.

How to get picked for netball

When you're trying to be noticed – whether it's to be picked for the netball team or to have your voice heard over the rabble – you've got to play up your outstanding qualities.

The first is to show your enthusiasm. If you look as though you're really pleased to be with certain people and eager to join in, it's more likely that they will include you in their activities.

The second is to look confident. If you look as though you can do the job, you'll get hired. If you look like the goal-scoring type, you'll be on the team.

The third is to be relaxed. If you look desperate or scared to death, you'll frighten people off. The trick is to appear enthusiastic *and* confident *and* cool all at the same time. This isn't easy, so learn the following and you'll never be stranded on the sidelines of life, or left warming the benches at netball.

1 Be up front

Just as the selection process begins, make your way to the front of the group. Don't waste your front row opportunity by slouching, chewing your nails or counting holes in the ozone. Stand tall and face the bods who are going eeny-meeny-miny-mo.

If you stand at the back you'll look like you're hiding and don't want to be chosen.

2 Posed for action

Stand with your feet slightly apart and with your hands on your hips. This makes you look stronger, fitter and more athletic. It also helps heaps if you're dressed appropriately. It might just be a malicious rumour but I have heard that trainers and super-short pleated skirts are a real turn-on for boys. Did I hear wrong?

3 Warm up

Jog on the spot or go through a limbering-up routine. Finish by gleefully rubbing your hands together. This gesture is saying: 'Come on coach, let me strut my stuff.'

If this routine is totally out of character for you or you think it makes you look just a little too eager, stand on the balls of your feet (makes you look taller) and rock slightly.

4 The look

57

Look the selector in the eye and smile. To avoid the choose-me-I'm-desperate grin think about your favourite things: skiing holidays, powder snow and an empty piste, or double-dating with P.J. and Duncan (Well, maybe not.).

6 Knowing the rules comes in handy

If you want to play netball (or get involved in any sort of activity, for that matter), then knowing how to play or what to do is a definite advantage. Not only will it *make* you more confident, you will *look* more confident. The fact that you've gone to the bother of learning the rules, is also proof of your enthusiasm.

Shrugging off shyness

Some people seem to have been born into this world with the ability to talk to absolute strangers. Me, I was giving instructions to the midwife the moment I popped out. ('Hurry up and get me washed and weighed I've got an interview to do.") But an equal number of people just clam up, unable to utter a nervous 'Hi" when they walk into a room. At a party these bods head straight for the wallpaper and spend the whole evening imitating a Laura Ashley floral print. If anyone (especially a potential boyfriend) dares to infiltrate their personal space and start a conversation they titter nervously, stare at their shoes and pull their head turtle-like into their shoulder-blades. If they were to meet this guy a couple of

58

times there would be no problem, but shyness discourages people from making a second attempt at breaking the ice. End of potential romance.

To break the vicious cycle of shyness, use 'Shalaa!' Not a patented anti-shy serum but an acronym for **s**mile, **h**ead up, **a**ct, **l**ips, **a**nkles and **a**sk.

Smile: you're never fully dressed without one, and apparently the moment you crack one your brain will send instructions for the production of happy hormones. So, strike a cheesy NOW!

Head up: try and get hold of a copy of the Madonna video for 'Papa Don't Preach'. In it Madonna goes to meet her passion and is obviously painfully shy when she sees him. She's so bashful she can hardly do more than look at the floor, until she catches a glimpse of herself. Realising that she looks like a total wuss she lifts her head and looks directly at her boyfriend. Immediately she changes from shrinking violet to towering sunflower. Whenever you're feeling shy, lift that head up and think of sunflowers!

Act: remember what the television presenter said about pretending to be highly in demand? Remember how I tried it and it worked? Well, it'll work for you too.

When you're feeling terribly bashful, imagine yourself as an actress who has been cast to play you in a film. For example, pretend you're Michelle Pfeiffer starring as you in a film about your life. In the scene where you (a beautiful and intelligent creature) walk into a room full of strangers, play it as Pfeiffer would. Would Pfeiffer head for the 'Ladies' or would she confidently charm the pants off everyone? Yep, that's right – she'd charm the Sloggi's.

Body consciousness raising

60

Close your eyes and imagine yourself at a party. You're being incredibly funny, witty, and bright and haven't spilled a thing all evening. Replay this scene as often as you like. Your self-image will improve tenfold.

Lips: an obvious sign of nervousness is lip-biting and finger-sucking. You can hold your head so high that it rubs against

the ceiling, but if your teeth are clamped around your lips or digits you'll look like a very tall three-year-old.

Ankles: Do you suffer from locked ankles? Have problems with tortuous ankle wrap? You need a dose of confidence. One dose of self-assurance and anxious ankles will be a thing of the past.

Anxious ankles is a common girlie posture problem and indicates that we girls are repressed (not something that has to be ironed twice) and doing our utmost to hide. We naively think that when we cross our ankles we become invisible. Wrong! All we are doing is showing just how up-tight we are.

61

Modelling agencies clicked onto this fact, and made a big deal of telling their models not to cross their ankles in case an interviewing client gets the impression that the model is too shy for the job.

Ask: If you're at a party and find yourself being forced into conversation, don't panic because you can't think of anything funny or controversial to say. The only thing you have to do is ask questions. And if these questions give the other person a chance to talk about themselves, all the better. This means that the burden of making with the sparkling chit-chat falls on their shoulders, not yours. And, oh, by the way they will be

chuffed that you're so interested in them. Like we said before, it's all to do with confidence trickery.

So that's shyness dealt with – almost. There's one more thing I'd like to mention. If ever you hear someone clearing their throat, it's usually because they're nervous. Next time you catch yourself clearing your throat, try to work out if you are doing it because you have a froggy throat or because you're a little shy. Either way, grab yourself a glass of water. It will help clear your throat and disguise your nervousness.

Backing-off bozos

All bullies and bozos (B&Bs) are cowards who use B.L. know-how for evil. Without their subtle grasp of the fundamentals of B.L., bullies would be revealed for the nerds they are.

If you're a victim of bullying you should probably be flattered (you're obviously important enough to be a threat), but I know, having been on the receiving end of such nastiness, that being an object of envy isn't any consolation at all.

Nobody deserves to be bullied. Even if you stood in front of a bozo with your tongue out and your thumbs stuck in your ears, it still doesn't give them the right to terrorise you.

B&Bs pick their victims carefully. They only harass people who are not likely to fight back, and are a good few inches shorter and pounds lighter than themselves. To outwit the B&Bs use your B.L. skills to dazzle them with your quiet confidence.

Tips to beat the bozos

☞ Imagine that there is an invisible thread running from cloud nine to the top of your head. When the resident of cloud nine gently pulls on the thread you become taller and taller, and your head is held higher and higher.

☞ If confronted by a bozo, smile in a friendly way. It will disarm the bozo – they expect their victims to look scared.

☞ Stand feet astride with your hands on your hips. This will help make you look larger and more confident.

☞ If you get into an argument with a bozo, don't point at them. (You know how annoyed you get when your parents do it. Point at a bozo and they'll go ballistic.) Instead, hammer home your argument by pushing your opened hands, palms down, toward the ground. Down-turned palms are a sign of authority and

show confidence. It is not an aggressive gesture.

☞ If you're in the classroom and you're being hassled, straddle your chair, using its back as a barrier for your chest. (It's almost like a substitute for a shield!).

If a bozo is using their chair in this way, stand behind him or her and take advantage of their 'unprotected' back. Don't stand too close or your action will be taken as menacing. And let's face it, you're not the bullying type.

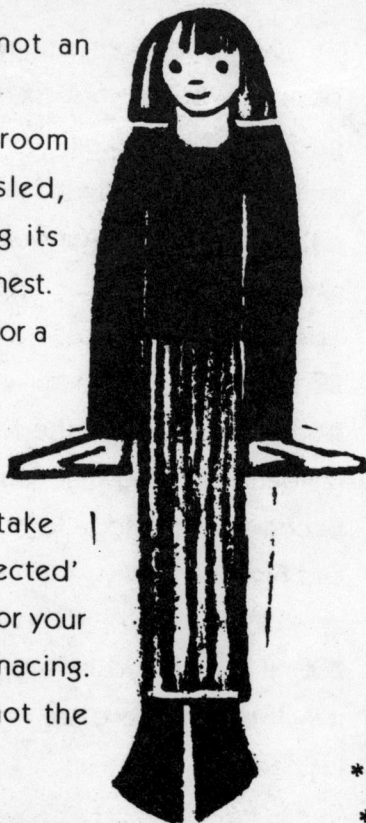

64

Bozo Alert

If you're ever being bullied, tell your friends, tell your teachers and above all, tell your parents.
DON'T be tempted to fight back.

Chapter Six

Dealing with Grown-Ups

(Mums and teachers, especially)

Emergency! Emergency! You're in the midst of a crisis – a do-or-die situation – which could end with you either a) having a great time and earning much credibility, or b) having a miserable time and never being able to raise your head in public again.

One of your mates is having an all-night party and you want to go. Trouble is, you're curfewed. You and your parents have come to an understanding that, no matter what day of the week, you will be inside your own front door by 11 pm. This is a non-negotiable, cast-iron contract. Breaking the curfew is punishable by television deprivation for the rest of your life.

Your pal Helen is allowed to stay at the party until 2 am, Sarah can stay all night, and even drippy Wendy doesn't have to be home until midnight. Help! You need a curfew extension! You need to ask your mum (or dad) for a major favour!

How are you going to do it?

Never fear B.L. is here!

By the end of this chapter you will have learned when *not* to make your move (in other words, you will be able to judge when your mum's in a bad mood), the best time to ask for a favour (like when your mum's receptive to novel thoughts and plea bargaining), and how to do it. I will also show you how to send out the right messages using B.L. magic. In short, you will be a Machiavelli of mum manipulation.

The same clever kit of tactics can be used on anyone – dad, siblings, teachers, employers, and most importantly the man at the ice rink. (You do want to get an extra hour on the ice, don't you?)

It's a bad time to ask mum for a favour when her....

☞ arms are folded over her chest – Your mum is telling you that she's in a negative frame of mind. But because some mums are permanently on the defensive, you may have to run the risk of incurring her wrath and say your piece. My fingers are crossed. I wish you luck.

67

hostile

☞ arms are crossed and her hands are clenched – Forget it! You are looking at one hostile person. Your mum is desperately trying to hold back a negative attitude. Her clenched hands are a mammoth sign of the grumps.

There are three degrees of the grumps:

Third degree grump: clenched hands resting on the table top or beating a steady rhythm on her thighs. If you know you have done nothing naughty in the past 24 hours, you could ask what's bugging her. But whatever you do, don't ask for a favour.

Second degree grump: her clenched hands are folded over her chest or resting on her hips. Make like you made a wrong turn and weren't really coming to see her. As you reverse out of the danger zone, mutter something like: 'I couldn't find my way out of a paper bag without a map.'

First degree grump: her clenched hands are supporting her chin, pushed deeply into her cheeks or covering her eyes. Good time for you to go out.

☞ lips are closed tight – Because mums are under immense amounts of stress everyday they learn to repress their emotions. Let's face it, if they exploded every time something went wrong you could stick them on a cliff and employ them as energy efficient lighthouses. To keep on smiling while every fibre of their body is seething means that

mums are great actresses. Like the Queen, they keep a stiff upper lip (literally) when it comes to keeping the lid on their deep-down feelings. So when you see your mum keeping a stiff upper lip, it's time to beat a retreat.

Bid her farewell if her tongue looks as though it is trying to punch a hole in her cheek. Your mum is ready to let rip, and one word from you could release a torrent of pent-up fury.

☞ chin is on her chest – This woman is down in the dumps. You have more chance of winning the Lottery than getting a positive response from her at the moment. (You'll be lucky if you get any response at all!) Instead, why don't you say something like: 'By heck, you're looking gorgeous today,' and then offer to make her a cup of tea.

So when is it a good time to ask mum for a favour?

Some sceptics feel that the time is never right for asking mum a favour. I disagree. Even the most over-stressed mum has a tiny window during her waking hours (a sleeping mum is strictly out of bounds) when all is well with the world. Yes, for an all-too-brief time every day your mama will be simultaneously happy, laid-back and unhassled. Ah, but how do you spot these blessed moments? Read on for enlightenment.

She's happy when she's smiling! Her mouth is relaxed (a tight-lipped smile is a dead giveaway for repressed nasty thoughts) and her eyes are sparkling. A true smile means happy eyes. If she's laughing, then count your lucky stars – your chances of wish-fulfillment are great.

She's laid back when her shoulders are relaxed and she's sitting in an open position (no crossed arms or legs) and, erm, dad's football team has just beaten the Cup favourites. It's always a good idea to ask favours when victory is in the air.

She's unhassled when she holds her head high and her shoulders are back. (If she's hassled, she won't be thinking about maintaining a good posture.) Head held proud is saying: 'I'm willing to listen and learn,' and if she showers you with full-eye contact you've also won her attention. So, go ahead and ask – you've got nothing to lose but a great night out.

Knowing when to stop

You're half-way through your speech and ready to launch into the heart-wrenching bit about how dropping the curfew would improve the lives of ten million homeless bunny rabbits in Outer Mongolia when you sense a change in the atmosphere. You suddenly realise that she's not falling for your well-rehearsed spiel. Out goes the positive aura, in comes the chill winds of a bummer one.

If you spot any of the following, your mum has rumbled you; you're on to a loser. Give up now and live to a ripe old age, or continue and suffer a horrible death by prolonged exposure to parental lecturing.

Oh, oh! She's picking lint

The moment your mother thinks that picking the lint and fluff off her cardie is more important (or more interesting) than what you've got to say, is the exact moment when you should stop talking.

Lint picking also means that your mother does not like what she's hearing. You can try to rescue the situation by stretching your palm-up hands (sign of honesty) towards her saying: 'C'mon mum. I can see you're not happy with this. Why?' It's a neat line that sometimes works, but you'd better prepare yourself for an early evening and total loss of credibility. Sorry.

71

She's peering over her glasses!

If this is the case, then all is not lost. Your mum is definitely dubious about your 'I'll just die if I can't stay till late' proposal and is looking over her specs to let you know.

What you've got to do is find a new way of winning her over, and years of painful experience tell me that the 'All my friends are staying late' argument is not the one to try.

Note: Non-spectacle wearers give the dubious look by peering at you through half-closed eyes. Decidedly unattractive.

Hell, she's rubbing her ears!

You didn't *really* have your heart set on staying out late, did you? If you did, tough. Your mum's rubbing her ears to let you know she's heard enough. Give up the cause. Better luck next time.

Oh, help! She's scratching her neck

Neck scratching isn't as bad as ear rubbing. Now that's a relief, isn't it? Neck scratching either means that your mum has an itchy neck (duh!) or she's still weighing up the pros and cons of your argument. You're obviously on the right track, so keep doing your stuff. I'm behind you all the way.

Jury's out – she's rubbing her chin

You know your mum's making her decision when she slowly strokes or taps her chin with her fingers. When she stops tapping or rubbing she's going to deliver her judgement. I hope for your sake that her decision is the right one!

Teacher tactics

Body language plays a mega role in the classroom. About half the things that you want to say to your teachers, and many of the things they want to say to you, are communicated using B.L.

For example, while your teacher is busy explaining number patterns to Sally in the first row, she glimpses your hand waving wildly about in the air. Without interrupting her explanation, she looks inquiringly at you. You then make the appropriate facial expressions of one who is busting to go to the loo. Teacher gets your message, nods her head and points to the door. You leap from your seat and charge from the room. During this entire 'conversation' neither of you said a word to each other, and the teacher didn't stop talking to Sally. Amazing, huh?

You also need B.L. know-how in order to establish relationships with your teachers. Not the sort of relationship which leads to sending each other

73

birthday cards, but the sort which lets you read your teacher's stress level. If you can tell when your teacher is at breaking point, then you'll know that it's not the time to ask for a homework extension. Not only will you be able to judge their mood, you'll be able to measure it: slightly ticked off, moderately grouchy, well-peeved, serious humour loss etc. By being so astute (another way of saying manipulative) you'll never end up in your teacher's bad books.

Body Alert

The grouch scale is a great way to skirt the halls of detention, but the best way to avoid teacher trouble is by not getting into trouble in the first place. Boring, I know, but true.

74

The grouch scale

How to use: watch your teacher carefully and match their body talk to its meaning on the following chart. Then read the invariably bad news in the 'Your plight' column and take heed of the words of comfort and advice.

The lower the grouch scale number, the better the mood. A reading of eight on the scale is very, very bad. You've got my sympathy.

GROUCH SCALE	TEACHER BODY TALK	MEANING	YOUR PLIGHT
1	One eyebrow raised, major eye contact.	Teacher isn't so much angry as bemused. You've done something which confirms what the teacher has always suspected – you're one slice short of a loaf.	Apologise and look very, very sad. Lower your head till your chin touches your chest.
2	Rubs or covers eyes.	Teacher is so tired of your behaviour that he or she can't bear the sight of you.	Stop whatever you're doing, shake your head a little as though you are knocking some sense into yourself, and do what you're supposed to be doing. An alternative tactic is to keep quiet, behave and avoid going anywhere near your teacher for the rest of the day. Do these things and all will be well.

75

GROUCH SCALE	TEACHER BODY TALK	MEANING	YOUR PLIGHT
3	Neck rubbing.	You're looking at a stressed example of the teacher species. If he or she slaps their neck before rubbing, stress has bubbled over into frustration. Your teacher is truly fed up.	Keep your head below the parapet, and don't put a foot wrong.
4	Head slapping.	Literal translation: 'Oh, not again!' Often means that the teacher is angry with themselves, but usually teacher is ticked off with you.	Prepare for a lecture. Teacher may give you a chance to explain your behaviour.
5	Tight lips, mean frown, hard eyes.	Er...does the word 'mad' ring any bells?	Longer, louder lecture coming your way. Only use your mouth for breathing.
6	Desk banging.	The louder the bang, the greater the temper. If the teacher also rises to their full height, he or she is showing their authority in an 'I dare you' gesture. Teacher is angry.	Don't even think of giving the 'I dare you' look in return. Take whatever comes without a murmur. You never know, you could end up enjoying detention.

GROUCH SCALE	TEACHER BODY TALK	MEANING	YOUR PLIGHT
7	Teacher is leaning over your desk, eyes fixed, no expression.	Six inches from your nose is a seriously unhinged person. Worse still is the total lack of any facial expression. This makes it impossible to guess what's in store for you. Needless to say, it won't be pleasant.	You're not going home on the 2.30 bus. Also a cert that the matter will be brought to the attention of the Head and your parents. Be humble and grovel a lot. This is not the time to try toughing it out.

unhinged

77

| 8 | As in 7, but your teacher is so close you can count the chicken pox scars. There is also steam coming from his or her ears. | Worst case. Teacher's fury knows no bounds. By lunchtime the whole school will know. Seismologists in Japan are waiting to measure the shock waves. Polynesians are evacuating the coast to avoid the tidal wave. Even cockroaches are finding somewhere safe to hide. | Sorry, there's not a thing you can do, except never do whatever you did again. Oh, and by the way, is this the first time you've been expelled? |

Use B.L. to get out of detention

You know how much trouble you're in, now work out what steps you have to take to minimise the damage.

The big secret is to appeal to the loving and caring side of your teacher's psyche. What you're after is the sympathy vote. To find your teacher's soft spot, follow these three steps.

Note: These techniques also work on parents.

STEP ONE: Make yourself look small and weak.

In the animal kingdom this strategy wouldn't work, because your attacker would simply think 'Oh, goody-goody, I can kill this one easily' and go for you with his incisors. However, in the human world vulnerability arouses protective instincts. While your teacher might not pat

78

you on the head and say 'There, there little one,' he or she may lower their voice and stop shaking their fist when they realise how scared you are.

To get the defenceless look, lower your shoulders and head, and clasp your hands to your chest like a frightened dormouse. Helps heaps if you can flash a pair of tear-filled innocent eyes in their direction and make your bottom lip quiver.

Body Alert

Step 1 can also be used when you want to look so frail that a vigorous gym session would be totally out of the question.

79

STEP TWO: 'Oh, I'm *soooo* ashamed!'
Stop all eye contact and, if physically possible, lower your head and shoulders even further. By doing this you're saying to the teacher: 'I'm so ashamed, I can't even bear to look into your accusing eyes.'

STEP THREE: Honest Jane lives again.
This final ploy should win you an Oscar nomination or, better still, less time in the sin bin.

Your teacher will have by now encouraged you to tell your side of the story, and may I recommend that you use the George Washington approach – the truth and nothing but the truth.

George Washington was the honest thief who became a U.S. President. When confronted about stealing apples from an orchard, good old George said: 'I cannot tell a lie, it was I!' (George, of course, also employed steps one and two. How else do you think he made it to the White House?)

When confessing *and* apologising *and* promising on a stack of 'Just Seventeen' magazines that you'll never commit such a heinous crime again, make sure that your Honest Jane hands are open and the palms exposed. In all probability your teacher will be so moved by your performance that he or she will be feeling guilty for having upset you. If not – hey, it was worth a try, wasn't it?

That's the serious stuff out of the way. Next stop, fun city! Is Michael Hutchence really in love with *that* woman? Does the dragon next door really dream of being a Bond Girl? You're about to find out!

Chapter Seven

The Body Game

No dice required

You are now passionately in awe of the power of body language, and brimming with ideas about how to employ it. But before we hit the streets to play some giggle-guaranteed body games, let's look at what we've found out about the lingo of the limbs.

You have learned how to:

1. become immensely popular.
2. collect friends like they're Esso stamps.
3. work out whether certain boys yearn for you or, sadly, lust after your best friend.
4. enchant 101 chosen chappies to fall hopelessly in love with you.
5. be picked for the school netball team.
6. shrug-off shyness.
7. be a less attractive victim for bozos and bullies.
8. bewitch your mum and others in authority.
9. gauge the stress and anger level of your teachers.

Face it, female – you're now so powerful that if this were the Middle Ages you'd be burning on the stake, whilst the plebs and sceptics shouted 'Slap another witch on the barbie.'

Time now for a carefully-planned psychological break (a sort of Time Out bar you can't eat) in which we're going to have some B.L. fun with body games.

I spy with my little eye

These games won't hone your skills in buying and selling real estate nor will they tie you up in knots, but they will fine-tune your anthropological skills so that B.L. will become second nature.

These games are for real, not for the weak-willed, and you won't find them in any toy shop. There's no dice, no dares, no losers. I was told about these games by a friend of mine who works for 'The Government', spends heaps of time in trouble zones, and carries folders marked 'Top Secret'. Yep, you've guessed it – they come straight from the training manual for (whisper, whisper) spies.

Spies are taught to be astute observers of human behaviour so that they can suss the good guys from the bad guys. In short, they are taught to be nosey! Makes you wonder if the ever-so-snoopy Vera Duckworth studied at RADA or M.I.5. My guess is M.I.5.

Are you ready to peer through the net curtain, and check out Charlie? Are you willing to give over an afternoon doing something that's heaps of fun? Great, so let's get snooping.

83

Game 1: Celebrity spotting

The aim of the game: To find the real story behind the gloss, glam and sham of celebrity photographs. The winner is the first to ferret out the truth about any of the following: Hutchence, Gere, Copperfield, Depp and the break-up of 'Take That'.

You will need: The Sunday papers or any gossip rag, your common sense and this book. A sense of humour and a wild imagination also help.

The rules: Spend a good couple of hours ploughing through the paparazzi pictures in the Sunday papers making your own observations about the stories behind the pictures. Look at every gesture, and compare what you see with what the story says. Jot down your version of the facts and keep an eye on future gossip columns for new info about your celebs. Compare these stories against your predictions to see who's really the ace snoop.

I remember one particular paparazzi soon-to-be-married scoop which involved 'A Certain Pop Star' and 'A Supermodel'. The published picture of the 'happy couple' told a different story. The Pop Star, for instance, held his head at a shifty angle, was scratching his collar (a sure sign that he's telling a lie) and did not look directly at the camera or his girlfriend. As for The Supermodel, her shoulders were rounded, and despite her smile there was sadness in her eyes. A quick glance at the bottom of the picture showed that their feet were pointing away from each other. I took this to mean that they were heading in different directions. Anyone with a bit of basic B.L. knowledge could tell that wedding bells were not about to ring. Sure enough, a couple of months later the 'happy couple' separated. Amazing huh? Give it a shot yourself!

Game 2: Dudewatching

The aim of the game: Use your noggin to work out what's really going down in the lives of the men and women on the Clapham omnibus. People-watching is an exercise for the intellect which will help you become totally clued-up on people's emotions, thoughts and intentions. The winner is the one who can pick the The Real Happy Harrys from The Pretenders.

You will need: Somewhere safe and comfortable to sit, lots of passers-by and a packet of crisps.

The rules of the game: Station yourself in a safe public place (for example: a bus-stop, a café, or a shopping mall) and observe the peeps who walk by. Without alarming your subjects look at them closely – the way they move, what they're wearing and carrying, and how they look (happy, sad, bored, anxious, etc). Now write the story of their life.

Here's one I prepared earlier: A man wearing a well-worn tweed jacket, carrying a briefcase and sporting a not-too-smart haircut approaches. He walks proudly, but as he passes he looks at me over his glasses, raises one eyebrow, looks at his watch, sighs to himself, looks at his watch again and hurries away.

Who was this tweedy man? Where was he going? What does he do?

The look he gave was judgemental, and his stature gave the impression that he holds himself in some regard. Chances are he's in a position of some importance (the briefcase) and considers himself indispensable (checking his watch because it wouldn't do to be late). On the other hand, his clothes and hair painted a picture of a slightly dizzy character, not a City broker. My guess is that he was a teacher running slightly late for class. What do you think?

Game 3: Mood mistress

Aim of the game: You know that B.L. changes according to mood, but did you know that it works in the reverse? Adopt the pose of an uptight person and you'll begin to feel uptight. Look laid-back, feel laid-back. Act like a dork, feel like a dork.

In this game we are going to have some fun, fun, fun by learning how to change your mate's mood.

You will need: yourself, a wicked sense of humour, very little conscience, and a trusting mate.

How to play alone: Let's say you wake up in a foul mood and want to snap out of it. What you do is this: you go to the mirror and take a good look at yourself. Do you look like the Hunchback of Notre Dame? Are you frowning? Do your eyebrows hang like fat caterpillars over your eyelids? You find it hard, no doubt, to look at yourself. This is the B.L. of one very uptight and sad soul.

Now you have a choice:

a) You can go out into the world looking like this, scaring children and small fury creatures, or

b) You can change your mood to one of sweetness and light.

You have ten seconds in which to make your decision.

If you chose 'a', then I hope we never meet. If you sensibly picked 'b',

87

read on because you're obviously ready to take total control of your life.

To change your mood (and look heaps more attractive) lift up your head, pull your shoulders back, straighten your posture and smile. Don't you feel like a new person?

Check your position every couple of minutes to make sure you haven't slipped back into the slouch of the grouch.

How to play with a friend. In this sneaky version of the game, you have to alter the body position, and therefore the mood, of another person without your subject knowing.

For example, your friend is not a happy bunny – her arms are firmly folded over her chest, her head is lowered and she's looking at you through half-closed eyes. Your mission (should you accept it) is to get her to raise her head and unlock her arms. How do you do it? You could get her to help you carry a couple of shopping bags (she'll have to uncross her arms then, won't she?), or you could ask her to get something from a high shelf. To do it she'll have to uncross her arms and raise her head. The moment her defences are down you must steam in with some cheery news or a joke or two. You'll be amazed at just how quickly your friend's mood will change.

Game 4: Animal magic

Aim of the game: To tell the temperature by watching your cat. (Surely it's easier to watch the weather report, isn't it?)

By closely studying animal behaviour you will understand human behaviour much better. An animal's body language is as intricate as a human's, but far simpler to interpret. Read any of Desmond Morris's books about vertebrate behaviour (the goings-on of any living creature with a backbone) and you'll find that human B.L. owes a great deal to the animal kingdom. Tarzan's manly chest thumping, for example, is straight from the apes. And all that courtship preening we do in front of our man also comes from the wild animal kingdom.

To study animal behaviour spend a day at the zoo and concentrate on only one enclosure – monkeys are especially good value. See if you can detect when it's

89

almost feeding time by noting the changes in behaviour. Can you spot the dominant male by reading his body language? Can you tell which monkey drinks PG Tips?

Because the whole concept of telling the temperature by watching your cat is just so weird, I'm going to tell you how to do it. It will also give you stay-at-home types something exciting to do.

You will need: A cat (surprise, surprise), a camera (Polaroid, if possible), and a thermometer.

How to play: Take pictures of your cat at each of the following temperatures (you'll need a thermometer to do this): 50-55 degrees F, 55-60 degrees F, 60-65 degrees F, 65-70 degrees F, and over 70 degrees F.

Your cat should be catching 20 winks on each occasion, and it's important that your feline be snoozing in the same place each time.

When you've got your photos (if your cat's anything like mine, it'll take you months) stick them in sequence from lowest temperature to highest on a piece of card and write the temperatures underneath.

What you should notice is that at low temperatures your cat sleeps curled up in a tight ball. In warmer weather it stretches out.

So the next time you want to know the temperature just watch the puddy-cat.

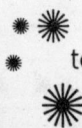

Game 5: Walk in another woman's shoes

The aim of the game: To see the effect that clothes have on your mood and B.L.

Our old friend Meg Ryan discovered that her whole persona changed when she donned '50s gear for the movie 'IQ'. As soon as she slipped on a tight, calf-length skirt and boob-hugging sweater she became a different woman. Her normally large bold strides were replaced by small ones. The lift-and-separate bra and girdle made her very conscious of her body and what she did with it. Her prim and proper haircut and strong make-up made her feel like a right little madam.

It's the same when we get dolled-up for a date. Once we've tossed the muck-around clothes on the floor, and stepped into something slinky, our whole attitude to life changes. We slip out of the humdrum state (in B.L. terms: semi-expressionless and slouching) and into a state of excitement (in

91

B.L. terms: sparkling eyes and muscles flexed for action).

So like someone almost said: clothes maketh the woman.

You will need: A whole pile of begged or borrowed clothes, a large mirror, a notebook and a whole afternoon. (Once you start this game it's very hard to stop.)

92

How to play: Try on different outfits and don't hold back on the make-up and accessories. See what happens when you wear fitted or loose clothes, high fashion or dross, old or new, bright or dark colours, patterns or plains. For every new creation jot down how you feel (for example: frumpy, sexy, prim, intelligent), and work out what it is about the outfit that changes your B.L. Do stilettos give you confidence because they make you taller? Do bright colours make you smile?

If you feel like a proper berk playing dress-up at your age, just remember that actresses do it all the time. You're in great company.

Chapter Eight

Truth Detective for Hire

Farewell to fibbers

Liar, liar your bot's on fire! (Sigh.) If only.

If a liar's bottom did burst into flame every time they murmured a porkie, life would be so much easier. Imagine all the pain and anguish we would be spared if everyone told the truth. Scotland Yard would be able to crack crimes effortlessly ('Listen, fella, if you don't start telling me the truth your butt will be bacon!') and personal hygiene dilemmas just wouldn't exist ('Jenny, you've got B.O and your breath stinks. So deal with them.Okay?').

If honesty ruled and fibbers fizzled we could all say goodbye to: malicious gossip, Lying Lizards who speak with forked tongue, two-timing scoundrels, and padded Wonderbras.

Crime crackers (the badged, not the salted kind) can tell when they are being fed a fib. The moment a criminal utters a porkie, his or her brain registers the deceit, setting off a series of chemical reactions throughout their body: their blood temperature may rise, certain hormones will be released, and their muscles may tense. Lie detector machines can monitor and measure these changes and pinpoint the lies.

Unfortunately for us amateur sleuths, spotting the fibbers isn't as easy as spotting smoke signals, and in the event that you didn't get a lie detector kit for Christmas, then the tips for sussing liars will come in dead handy.

94

Body Alert

The flip side of knowing how to spot lies is, of course, knowing how to hide them. Not that you would ever tell porkies.

Ten tips for sussing liars

Question 1: Is suspect pulling at his or her collar?

If you've ever heard the phrase 'hot under the collar' and know what it means, go to the top of class. If someone is lying they will subconsciously tug at their collar or run their fingers around

the inside of the collar as if it has suddenly become four sizes too small. What's happened is that the brain has become really peeved at being made an accomplice to a lie, and to get back at the fibber has engineered a hot flush. This causes the scoundrel to sweat, making his collar sticky and unbearably uncomfortable. The suspect is squirming, Gov. It won't be long before he or she tells you the truth.

Question 2: Is suspect covering mouth with hand?

When your mum told you to put your hand over your mouth it was to stop you sneezing germs all over her and anyone else within a two-metre radius. When a fibber hides their mouth they're not thinking about their germ count, only their lie count. Yep, our poor old suspect is so ashamed of what he or she is saying, they hope that by covering their mouth it will tone down the lie. Is that stupid or is that stupid?

If you're not sure it's a porkie, get the suspect to repeat their answer (their lie) and watch them carefully. If their hand automatically goes to their mouth, the suspect is pulling the wool over your eyes.

Question 3: Is suspect touching their nose?

Nose-touching is a sophisticated version of mouth-hiding. It's as if the suspect is trying to cover-up the cover-up. If he or she puts a hand to their mouth they know their lie will be spotted, so instead they touch their nose. But as usual, Sherlock, you are one B.L. step ahead and know exactly what sort of sneaky game they're playing.

Question 4: Is suspect rubbing eyes?

There's an old legend (read 'absolute whopper') about three wise monkeys. The first monkey kept a hand

firmly plastered over his mouth so that he could speak no evil, the second kept his hands over his ears so that he could hear no evil and the third covered his eyes so that he could see no evil. Interesting, huh, but an almost pointless literary diversion, except for the third 'see no evil' monkey.

When a person (or a monkey) rubs their eyes they are trying not to 'see' the lie they have just created. Believe it or not, even liars can be ashamed of their disgusting behaviour.

Question 5: Is suspect making horrible swallowing noises?

Remember when we looked at confidence building, I mentioned that a froggy throat was a sign of

97

croak beautiful hat

nervousness and that you should try to put a stop to it? Yeah. Well there's another reason for putting the lid on these ugly utterances – they can indicate that you're telling a lie.

The brain, once again acting as the good guy, sends out messages to the rest of the body saying: 'Rotter's lied. Tighten neck muscles immediately.' The tightening of the muscles in the neck causes the fibber to swallow heavily and to make noises like the toad they are. (Honest people have cute little green tree frogs in their throat; liars are home to great big ugly warty cane toads. Yeuk!)

98

If you only learn one thing in life, make sure it's this:

If they croak like a toad,
They're in lying mode.

Question 6: Is suspect blushing?

Everyone knows that blushing means that someone is embarrassed. Your knickers fall down – you blush; you bump into your main man – you blush; you tell a bare-faced fib – you blush big time.

When a fibber fibs, or even just thinks about it, their face and sometimes even their neck, turns beetroot red. Guilt is literally written all over his or her face so it should be dead-easy for you Truth Detectives to spot the whoppers.

Body Alert

Committed and practised liars may not be embarrassed by their lie and will, therefore, not blush. So before jumping to conclusions, think carefully about the personality of your subject. If you're dealing with someone who'd happily sell their mother for a handful of CD tokens, there's as much chance of them blushing as snow falling in the Sahara. To get to the truth you'll have to use one of the other tips.

Question 7: Does suspect look shifty?

In panto, when the evil Baron Loadsadosh takes to the stage he spends half an hour prancing around like a madman and giving shifty glances to the audience. He's doing this because he wants you to know that he's not the type of boy that you'd take home to meet your mum and dad. Shifty glances are THE undisputed sign of underhandedness.

Question 8: Does suspect look you in the eyes?

If he's a liar, I very much doubt it. Eyes are the windows of the soul and will give away the secrets our tongues refuse to speak.

Fibbers know this, so when they're telling a lie they avoid full-on eye contact. If you can't see their peepers, you can't spot the fib.

99

Question 9: Does suspect hide palms?

If you don't know why this is so important, you must have been boiling up the kettle in chapter two. Open palms are a sign of honesty. Hidden palms show that something (in this case, the truth) is being suppressed.

Question 10: Does suspect have dark curly hair, one green eye and one blue eye and is carrying five bags labelled 'Loot'?

If so, he's wanted by Sussex Police for grand larceny. Book 'im Danno!

Chapter Nine

Testing Times

Judge Dread and Interview Hell

Going through any sort of one-to-one interview is a dead scary experience. No matter how realistic you are about your chances of getting the job or course of your choice, it's very hard to be cool, calm and confident. Not only do you have to make intelligent conversation with a total stranger who is wearing a smart suit and is sitting barricaded behind a big desk, but you have to try your hardest to make the chap or chapess like you.

Over the next few years you are going to be confronted with the following sorts of interviews.

☞ Oral tests (or vivas) to determine whether you pass or fail an examination.

☞ An interview for a Saturday job which will give you the readies to buy a new sound centre or the necessary experience you need for a future career.

☞ The college interview to see if you're a suitable candidate for a place in the hallowed halls of learning.

Bare Fact

Interviews are like computer games. If you can suss the secret moves you get through them without exploding.

Welcome to Interview Hell, the most frightening virtual reality game to hit the computer world in the last five minutes. Can you steer past the snide remarks, keep your composure under rapid-fire questioning, ooze confidence in enemy territory and maintain full power under stress? Have you sussed which moves mean sudden death and those which guarantee victory?

103

I can hear your knees knocking together already. Calm down, you are about to be empowered. The instruction manual for Interview Hell will give you some control over how the interview game is played. (If you can totally manipulate the way the interview goes, you should be doing the interviewing.)

Body Alert

The instruction manual can help you perform at your best in an interview, but what you actually say is all up to you. So be a good scout and be prepared!

Interview Hell – the instruction manual

Every player (the interviewee) is given three weapons. The interviewer or examiner, on the other hand, has about a million sneaky weapons and questions tucked up their sleeve. Sorry.

WEAPON 1: KNOWLEDGE

If you're doing an oral exam and you've learned your stuff, you deserve to – and should – pass. Answer a question correctly and you'll get marks.

The same applies to a job interview. If you go to the trouble of finding something out about either the job or the company and can demonstrate your knowledge in the interview, you'll get 'marks' for it. Dead logical.

WEAPON 2: A CLEAR HEAD

A clear head gives you the ability to think quickly, speak clearly and to keep your head even when a shock horror question is thrown at you.

WEAPON 3: ATTITUDE

Show off the right qualities – enthusiasm, a pleasant persona, confidence and a willingness to learn – and the interviewer will be bowled over.

Let your body do some talking

When you go for an interview you can leave all the talking to your mouth (with brain attached) or you can let your body do some communicating as well.

Picture it this way: the interviewer has asked you a question and you're answering it like a pro. You're speaking clearly and your thoughts are logical and informed – very impressive. But what are you doing with your body? Your legs are swinging back and forth, your fingers are drumming nervously on the arm of the chair, and you've yet to make eye contact with the interviewer. Look, I don't want to be nasty or to let you down in your hour of need, but your body language stinks. Your chances of getting this job are going down the gurgler, so you'd better shape up your body act.

105

Do the following exercises and memorise the tips, and the world will be your interview oyster (or nut cutlet for vegetarians). Never again will a snotty French oral examiner or a smarmy besuited interviewer get the better of you. So go forth and get some control.

Body Alert

Be confident by all means, but don't be cocky or smart-mouthed – examiners and interviewers hate it.

Body consciousness raising: The French oral

Imagine you're an examiner and waiting outside your door is a dream pupil. This pupil is so good and works so hard she deserves to get an 'A'. You ask the student to come in, but just before she enters you try to imagine how she'll conduct herself. How will she greet you? Will she be smiling or scowling? How will she behave over the next 20 minutes of French oral purgatory? How will she sit? What will be her demeanour?

The true 'A' student will (tick the correct answers):

- ☐ Slouch
- ☐ Walk tall
- ☐ Smile
- ☐ Snarl
- ☐ Return a handshake and greeting
- ☐ Slap the examiner on the back and say 'How's things, buddy?'
- ☐ Sit slightly forward on the seat
- ☐ Rest their feet on the examiner's desk
- ☐ Hold their head high and make eye contact
- ☐ Roll their eyes around and look everywhere but at the examiner
- ☐ Chew their lips and sigh deeply at every question

- ☐ Fold their arms across their chest
- ☐ Rest their hands on their lap
- ☐ Answer confidently, clearly and slowly
- ☐ Mutter
- ☐ Leap out of the chair as soon as the last question is asked, and shout 'I thought you'd never finish!'
- ☐ Wait for the examiner to say they can leave

Body Alert

It's not what you know, but the way that you show it.

107

Body consciousness raising: The Saturday job

Imagine you are interviewing candidates for the job of casual cashier. An applicant walks in without knocking and cruises towards a chair on the far side of the room. On the way she inspects a couple of knick-knacks on a shelf. So far she hasn't said a word, nor looked you in the face. She drops herself into a chair, stretches out her legs and crosses them at the ankles. She rests her hands on her hips. To every question she gives a short abrupt answer and never once does she smile or look up. At the end of the interview she drags herself out of the chair and makes to leave, but as she gets to the door asks 'Well, do I get the job or not?'

What do you think? List your reasons for not giving this girl the job:

_____

_____

_____

_____

_____

_____

See, body language is really important.

While researching this book I spoke to three professional interviewers about the effect an applicant's posture, attitude and behaviour have on the interviewer. Here's what they had to say:

108

The college interview

"When I was interviewing applicants for the final place on a course, we ended up with two suitable candidates. Both had scored similar marks in the exams and had roughly the same amount of experience. There was little between them and I dreaded having to make the decision. Both girls fronted up for the final interview, and instead of being faced with a hard decision there was really no contest. One of the girls was extremely enthusiastic. She sat on the edge of her chair and had very searching, intelligent eyes. I gave the final place to her."

The casual job interview

"A few months ago we had a vacancy for a casual assistant at the bookshop. It's a great job because it gives the employee a chance to experience the book business at a grass roots level. We had lots of written applications and one seemed perfect. He wrote about his interest in books, and his letter was polite and intelligent and provided us with all the information we required. I was really disappointed when he came in for the interview. He leaned across the desk and was really 'in my face' when I talked to him. When he left he slapped me heartily on the back. I thought he was too cocky for the job."

The career job interview

"The job that had to be filled needed someone who would take initiative and be enthusiastic about new ideas. A lot of the people we interviewed were adequately qualified, but not one of them displayed the right mix of self-confidence and a willingness to learn. I'll know the perfect candidate when I *see* him or her."

In all three examples it is easy to see what the interviewers are looking for: confidence (in what you know, or your ability to do a job), a pleasant personality (not pushy or arrogant, but easy to get on with), enthusiasm (your desire to get the job and do it) and respect (for the interviewer and for yourself). What isn't mentioned in these comments is that interviewers are also looking for honesty. You might try to pass off an itty-bitty white lie, but the interviewer won't be fooled. Your lie might sound convincing, but your B.L. will give you away.

Body consciousness raising

Think about the comments of the career job interviewer and work out which body moves would signal confidence and a willingness to learn.

The perfect candidate

Imagine you're in the reception area of Paperclips and Sticky Things International. The Personnel Manager (P.M.) has just walked into the crowded room, looked around, spotted an eager face and said 'Miss Thingummy?' (That's you, by the way!)

You stand up (to show respect), look the P.M. straight in the eye (shows that you're confident and honest), smile and say 'Hello' (not only polite, but friendly). You then offer, or return a handshake.

Body Alert

The handshake is very important. This is the first and maybe the only time you'll have physical contact with your interviewer so you have to use it to demonstrate what you're made of.

If your handshake grip is too firm, the interviewer may get the impression that you're a domineering character – a bit of a tough gal. If it's sloppy and, erm, sweaty (a bit like a wet warm fish) it may be read that you're nervous and unsure of yourself.

Make sure your handshake is like you: confident and on the mark!

112

The P.M. will show you to his or her office and invite you to sit down. Never sit down until you're asked, otherwise you show disrespect and may appear too casual or too pushy. Sit up straight, feet planted on the floor and place your hands on your lap. Whatever you do, don't apply a white-knuckle grip to the arm of the chair – it will look like you're getting ready for the triple corkscrew ride at Alton Towers. Keep your head up (shows a positive attitude), listen, and look interested *and* interesting.

To demonstrate a point gently press the tips of your fingers together to form a steeple (that's why this B.L. move is called 'steepling'). Keep your hands low;

hold them too high and it looks like you're trying to teach the interviewer to suck eggs.

Show some respect

You will have noticed that the P.M. takes a dominant position. He or she will sit in a high-backed chair behind a desk, or perched on the edge of a desk. No, the P.M. is not necessarily a control freak, but he or she is letting you know that they are the boss. And as boss they want your respect. Show them some and they will realise that you know what the word 'hierarchy' means.

Try not to raise your head so high that you're looking down your nose at the P.M. (they will think you have ideas above your station). Also be careful to stay well out of their personal space. Remember how the boy in the book store rubbed his potential boss up the wrong way by getting 'in his face'? He also slapped his interviewer on the back. This is a friendly gesture, not a professional one! Steer clear!

P.S. Hierarchy is a posh word for pecking order.

Body Alert

I know you want to make 'friends' with this geezer, but now is not the time to start mirroring his movements. Do it and the P.M. will have security show you the door.

113

The pleasure of your company

How on earth do you look 'pleasant'? How do you show that you would be a delight to work with?

Well, for one, you turn up to your interview looking clean and smart. You also turn up on time. You mustn't grumble about the fact that you got hopelessly lost and as a result had to take three buses and walk two miles. You won't get any sympathy. Mention getting lost and the P.M. will suspect that you're not the most organised person on the planet. An organised and efficient bod would have checked out how to get to the interview without a hitch. If you do get lost, do yourself a favour and don't say a word about it.

114

The single most important B.L. signal is a smile. Don't smile constantly (your interviewer may think you're insane!), but just enough to show that you have a calm and pleasant nature. If, at the end of the interview, the interviewer remembers you as the girl with the smart answers *and* the sunny smile, you're likely to stand out as an attractive candidate.

Bright-eyed and bushy-tailed

Nothing to do with coming dressed as a squirrel, but everything to do with showing that you're nuts about the job. Go prepared knowing something about the job or the company. An interviewer will be tickled

pink to know that you've put in the effort to do some research. Clever you.

Whether you're talking or listening, reflect your interest by leaning forward and opening your eyes a little wider to show that you are stunned at the number of paperclips the company manufactures in a year. Before answering a question, let your eyes wander for a nano second as though in deep concentration. Not only do these simple gestures make you look good, they also let the interviewer think that they are doing a good job. Flattery will get you everywhere.

Honesty's the best policy

If you're asked a tricky question and feel that your answer isn't convincing, do the old trick of turning your palms upwards when you reply. This gesture is saying to the interviewer: 'Look, I'm not sure if my answer was right, but I'm only too happy for you to tell me the correct response.'

One simple bit of B.L. and you've convinced the interviewer that you're honest, open, frank and – cop this – willing to learn. What a girl!

Why are you nervous?

All these tips and you're still nervous? Don't worry! You're meant to be!

115

Interviews are designed to put you under a certain amount of pressure and are played out so that the interviewer appears to be much more important than you. If it all gets too much for you, just mentally knock the interviewer down a few pegs. Replace the suit with a pair of loud shorts and a tasteless shirt, and picture him or her sitting on the loo.

116

Make your interrogator human and you'll find that your performance becomes a lot more human and believable too.

Smile! you're on the telephone

You really think I've flipped this time, don't you? But I haven't because smiling on the phone works. It's especially important when you're making the initial contact with a potential boss.

Cast your mind back to when we were talking about changing your mood by changing your body language. Well, the same thing applies to your voice.

If you're smiling, then your voice will sound happy. Wear a frown, and your voice will sound down.

Chapter Ten

The Dictionary of B.L.

Moving meanings

You are now a fully-qualified anthropologist, a David Attenborough of the shopping mall. All you need now is some on-the-job training.

On the next few pages you'll find the dictionary of B.L. – the movement or gesture alongside its meaning.

Don't attempt to memorise this list, it's far better if you adopt a gesture and see what effect it has. Similarly, when you catch someone using a B.L. gesture take a mental note to compare what you thought it meant to its dictionary meaning. Before too long B.L. will become second nature and you'll no longer need to refer to this chapter. Everything you'll need will be at your fingertips (or in your head, at least)!

All over the globe thousands (maybe even hundreds of thousands) of diplomats, businessmen and women, interviewers, teachers and common folk like you and me are learning how to use body language. Some sociologists reckon that in the not too distant future so many people will be tuned into the language of bod that it will no longer be a 'secret weapon' but an accepted and common means of human communication.

Imagine it, space-age generations who are so intuitive and hypersensitive to the thoughts and emotions of others that the spoken word has become obsolete.

So get orbiting and become a B.L. expert before you get left behind in the inter-planetary scuffle!

Cheers! And here's looking at 'them'!

MESSAGE	BODY LANGUAGE
'I'm friendly.'	A smile.
'We see eye-to-eye.'	Full eye contact and a relaxed smile.
'I'm really *very* pleased to meet you again!'	Two-handed shake (page 27).
'I'm an honest person.'	Up-turned palms and open arms (page 28).
'You can come into my circle of friends!'	An 'open' body without barriers. Arms, legs or ankles uncrossed.
'I'm interested in what you're saying.'	Head tilted to one side while listening intently.

119

MESSAGE	BODY LANGUAGE
'I'm a likeable soul.'	Soft, warm voice.
'We're so similar.'	Mirroring (page 29).
'I'm giving you the eye!'	Lingering gaze that takes in your whole bod. Pupils dilated, blinking rapid.
'I want to be your best buddy.'	Moving into someone's personal space (page 35).
'I'm happy to see you.'	Flashing eyebrows.
'I want to look really good for you.'	Preening – running fingers through hair, smoothing clothing, straightening tie, applying make-up etc.

'You're the one that I want.'	Using knee, crossed leg or upper body to 'point' to a loved one.

MESSAGE	BODY LANGUAGE
'Move closer!'	Speaking in a whisper.
'Look into my eyes!'	Fluttering eyelashes or the slow two-eyed wink.
'Now you have me, now you don't.'	Attention-seeking ploy.

121

'I want to kiss you.'	Attracting attention to lips by gently biting or running the tongue over them.
'I really want you to fancy me!'	Displaying inside of wrists or revealing the nape of the neck.
'I'm being coy with you!'	Playing with hair and wearing the wide-eyed innocent look.

MESSAGE	BODY LANGUAGE
'I'm fit enough to love!'	Legs crossed and pointing toward the subject of passion (pages 39, 49).
'I'm really happy.'	Relaxed pose (page 70).
'I'm confident!'	Standing tall, shoulders back, chin up, eyes bright and gaze focused.
'I'm a reliable person.'	Feet apart.
'I'm strong!'	The Peter Pan pose: hands on hips and feet apart.
'I'm enthusiastic.'	Rubbing hands together with a happy gleam in the eyes. (Without the happy countenance you'll look like Scrooge who's clapped eyes on a penny.)
'I'm able and raring to go.'	Standing on balls of feet and rocking slightly.

MESSAGE	BODY LANGUAGE
'I'm nervous.'	Fingernail and lip biting. Naughty, naughty!
'I'm really nervous.'	Clearing throat constantly.
'I'm repressed and want to hide.'	Locked ankles (page 61).
'I'd rather you didn't get too close.'	Crossed arms and ankles. No eye contact.
'I mean what I say.'	Statement accompanied by hands (palm down) pushed toward the ground in a blocking motion (page 63).
'This is my shield.'	Sitting backwards astride a chair (page 64).

123

MESSAGE	BODY LANGUAGE
'I'm about to explode!'	Clenched fists (page 68).
'I'm in a negative mood.'	Tightly pursed lips, lowered head and rounded shoulders.
'I'm frustrated and holding back.'	Hands clenched together.
'I don't like what you're saying.'	Lint picking (page 71).
'I'm dubious.'	Peering over specs, or looking through half-closed eyes.
'I don't want to listen.'	Rubbing or covering ears.
'I'm not certain I agree.'	Neck scratching (page 72).
'I'm making up my mind.'	Stroking chin (page 73).
'I'm bemused.'	Raised eyebrows.
'I'm tired of this.'	Rubbing eyes.

124

MESSAGE	BODY LANGUAGE
'I'm stressed out.'	Rubbing neck. If neck is slapped first, then the person is stressed and angry.
'Oh, not again! This is all I need!'	Slapping forehead or cradling head in hands.
'I'm mad with you!'	Lowered eyebrows, a tense frown and a steely stare (page 77).
'I'm absolutely furious!'	Banging desk and then suddenly standing up. Expression will be fixed.
'I'm so ashamed.'	Avoiding eye contact and head lowered (page 79).
'I'm little and I'm scared.'	Rounded shoulders, hands clasped on chest, wide slightly teary-eyes.
'I'm honest.'	Big 'innocent' eyes, open palms and arms.

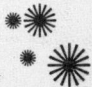

MESSAGE	BODY LANGUAGE
'I'm uncomfortable with what's happening.'	Pulling at collar or running fingers inside the collar (page 95).
'I'm not sure about what I'm saying. I could be lying!'	Hand over mouth when speaking, or touching nose (page 96).
'I don't want to witness these lies!'	Rubbing eyes or covering them.
'I'm nervous about what I'm saying. I could be lying!'	Swallowing noises (page 97).
'I'm finding it hard to tell a lie.'	Avoiding eye contact.
'I'm hiding something.'	Closed palms.
'I'm embarrassed.'	Blushing.
'I'm a bit of a rotter, and I'm checking to see if you're checking me.'	Shifty sideways glances.

MESSAGE	BODY LANGUAGE
'I'm about to say something important.'	Steepled hands.

MESSAGE	BODY LANGUAGE
'I'm better than you.'	Taking the dominant position (page 113).
'I'm so much better than you!'	Frequently closing eyes while talking.
'What on earth are you on about?'	Screwing up one side of the face.
'That's silly!'	Making like a prune and screwing up the whole face.

The nitty-gritty about the best books around

Am I Normal?
'Just Seventeen's' agony aunt, Anita Naik gives down-to-earth answers to all those awkward questions you've always wanted to ask, but never dared!

Families: can't live with them, can't live without them!
No one gets on with their nearest and dearest all the time – but, with help from Anita Naik, learning to live together may be easier than you think!

Is this Love?
From flirting and first dates to jealousy and break-ups, Anita Naik helps you handle all the ups and downs of love.

The 'Just Seventeen' Guide to being Gorgeous
Want to know how to make the most of what you've got? Adele Lovell gives the low-down on hair, skin, make-up, healthy eating and much more.

Stand up for Yourself!
Helen Benedict's book explains how to handle all kinds of problems which may crop up on the street or in the home. Essential reading for all young people who want to protect themselves without getting paranoid.

Don't just sit there – Get A Life!
Ever feel you're in a rut? Think you should be having more fun? If the answer's 'yes', you need this book! Victoria McCarthy shows how you can take control of your life and change it for the better.

Everything you ever wanted to know about periods... but didn't like to ask!
Charlotte Owen's essential book explains all you'll ever need to know about one of the most important times in your life.
Recommended by Brook Advisory Centres